EXPLORING SPACE

Earth

by Derek Zobel

Consultant:
Duane Quam, M.S. Physics
Chair, Minnesota State
Academic Science Standards
Writing Committee

BELLWETHER MEDIA • MINNEAPOLIS, MN

Note to Librarians, Teachers, and Parents:

Blastoff! Readers are carefully developed by literacy experts and combine standards-based content with developmentally appropriate text.

Level 1 provides the most support through repetition of high-frequency words, light text, predictable sentence patterns, and strong visual support.

Level 2 offers early readers a bit more challenge through varied simple sentences, increased text load, and less repetition of high-frequency words.

Level 3 advances early-fluent readers toward fluency through increased text and concept load, less reliance on visuals, longer sentences, and more literary language.

Level 4 builds reading stamina by providing more text per page, increased use of punctuation, greater variation in sentence patterns, and increasingly challenging vocabulary.

Level 5 encourages children to move from "learning to read" to "reading to learn" by providing even more text, varied writing styles, and less familiar topics.

Whichever book is right for your reader, Blastoff! Readers are the perfect books to build confidence and encourage a love of reading that will last a lifetime!

This edition first published in 2010 by Bellwether Media, Inc.

No part of this publication may be reproduced in whole or in part without written permission of the publisher. For information regarding permission, write to Bellwether Media, Inc., Attention: Permissions Department, 5357 Penn Avenue South, Minneapolis, MN 55419.

Library of Congress Cataloging-in-Publication Data

Zobel, Derek, 1983-
Earth / by Derek Zobel.
   p. cm. – (Blastoff! Readers. Exploring space)
Includes bibliographical references and index.
Summary: "Introductory text and full-color images explore the physical characteristics of the planet Earth. Intended for students in kindergarten through third grade"–Provided by publisher.
ISBN 978-1-60014-404-2 (hardcover : alk. paper)
1. Earth–Juvenile literature. I. Title.
QB631.4.Z63 2010
525–dc22
                        2009038453

Text copyright © 2010 by Bellwether Media, Inc.
Printed in the United States of America, North Mankato, MN.

010110   1149

Contents

Earth is a **planet** in the **solar system**. It is the only planet known to have life.

Earth

Earth is the third planet from the sun. It is 93 million miles (150 million kilometers) away from the sun.

All the planets in the
solar system **orbit** the sun.
The sun's **gravity** pulls on
the planets to keep them in orbit.

Earth completes
one orbit of the sun
in a year.

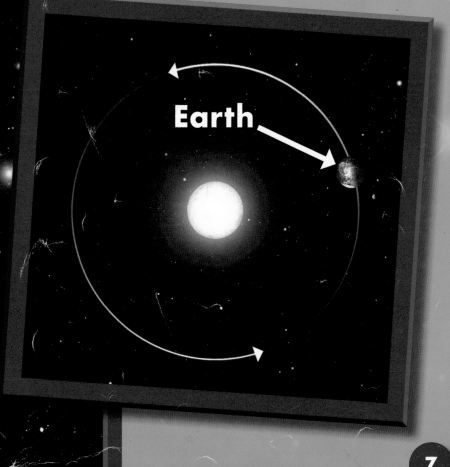

Earth

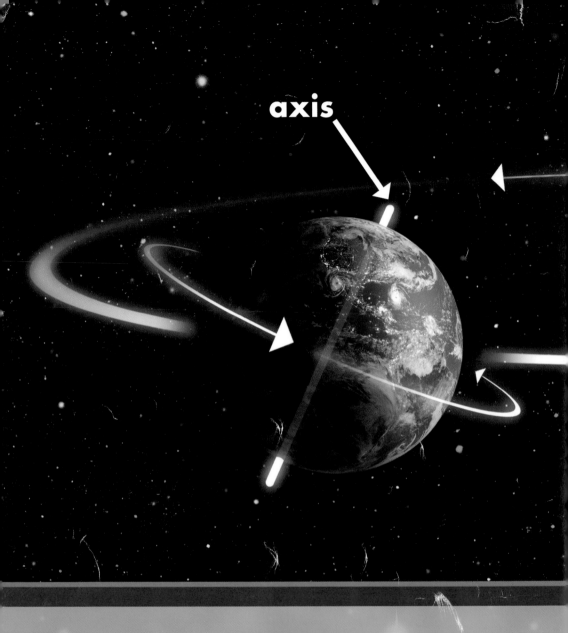

axis

Earth moves very fast in its orbit.
It travels at 66,700 miles
(107,000 kilometers) per hour!

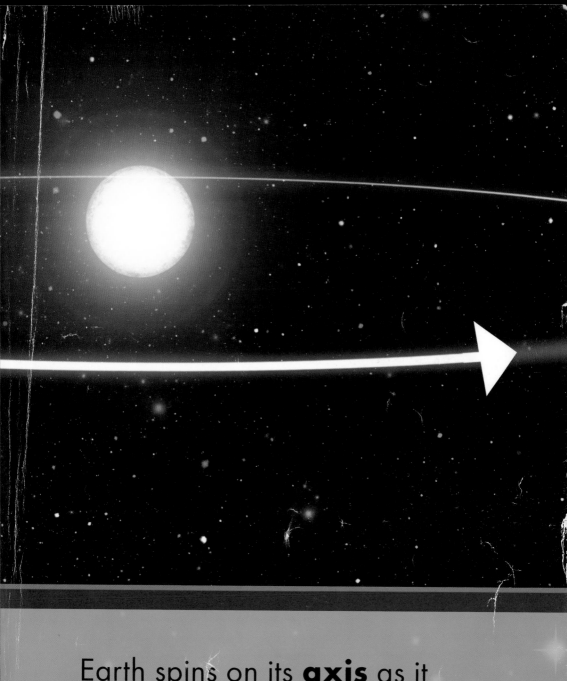

Earth spins on its **axis** as it
orbits the sun. One full spin of
Earth is called a day.

Over seventy percent of Earth's surface is covered with water. This includes rivers, lakes, oceans, and **glaciers**.

glacier

The large amount of
water on Earth allows
it to support life.

The rest of Earth's surface is land. The land has many features.

mountains

plains

canyons

jungles

deserts

Earth has mountains, plains, canyons, jungles, deserts, and other features.

Earth has a thick **atmosphere**.
It becomes thinner as **altitude**
increases. It reaches 370 miles (600
kilometers) above the Earth's surface.

The atmosphere is made of gases. One of those gases is **oxygen**. People and animals need to breathe oxygen to survive.

the moon

Earth has only one moon.
The moon orbits Earth.
Both Earth and the moon
orbit the sun.

Earth and the moon are about 238,900 miles (384,000 kilometers) apart.

Earth's gravity holds the moon in its orbit. The moon's gravity affects the oceans on Earth.

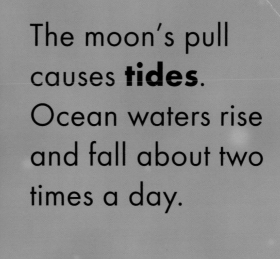

The moon's pull
causes **tides**.
Ocean waters rise
and fall about two
times a day.

Scientists know a lot about Earth. The land, the water, and the sky have all been explored.

However, there
will always be
more to learn
about the planet
we call home!

Glossary

altitude—the height above sea level on Earth

atmosphere—the gases around an object in space; Earth's atmosphere makes it possible for life to exist.

axis—an imaginary line that runs through the center of a planet; a planet spins on its axis.

glaciers—huge sheets of ice found in cold parts of Earth

gravity—the force that pulls objects toward each other; the sun has more gravity than any other object in the solar system.

orbit—to travel around the sun or other object in space

oxygen—a gas that people and animals need to breathe to survive

planet—a large, round space object that orbits the sun and is alone in its orbit

solar system—the sun and the objects that orbit it; the solar system has planets, moons, comets, and asteroids.

tides—the changes in sea level caused by the pull of the sun and moon on Earth's oceans

To Learn More

AT THE LIBRARY
Brimner, Larry Dane. *Earth*. New York, N.Y.: Children's Press, 1999.

Guilain, Charlotte. *Earth*. Chicago, Ill.: Heinemann Library, 2009.

Taylor-Butler, Christine. *Earth*. New York, N.Y.: Children's Press, 2008.

ON THE WEB
Learning more about Earth is as easy as 1, 2, 3.

1. Go to www.factsurfer.com.

2. Enter "Earth" into the search box.

3. Click the "Surf" button and you will see a list of related Web sites.

With factsurfer.com, finding more information is just a click away.

BLASTOFF! JIMMY CHALLENGE
Blastoff! Jimmy is hidden somewhere in this book. Can you find him? If you need help, you can find a hint at the bottom of page 24.

Index

Blastoff! Jimmy Challenge (from page 23).
Hint: Go to page 11 and search the world over.